The material was previously published in the book *Fearless Fair Isle Knitting 30 Gorgeous Original Sweaters, Socks Mittens, and More.* (ISBN 978-1-60085-327-2)

First published in this format 2012.

The Taunton Press
Inspiration for hands-on living®

The Taunton Press, Inc.
63 South Main Street, PO Box 5506
Newtown, CT 06470-5506

e-mail: tp@taunton.com

Interior design and Layout:
Chalkley Calderwood
Illustrator: Christine Erikson
Photographers: Alexandra Grablewski; except
pp. 25–31 © Nick Pharris

Printed in the United States of America
10 9 8 7 6 5 4 3 2 1

Table of Contents

Children's Dress

Get ready for spring with this adorable sleeveless summer dress. (Pictured at left knit in Decadent Fibers' hand-dyed, superwash sock yarn.) It's simple yet elegant, with a faced hem, ribbon trim, and applied I-cord edging and buttons.

Yarn   Superfine Weight Yarn (CYCA 1), approx. 800 (800, 1,200) yd. Natural; for all sizes, 400 yd. each of Bright Orange, Bright Yellow, Light Green, Dark Green

Note   *Hand-dyed yarns can sometimes bleed in the wash. Before knitting with them, wash hand-dyed yarns in separate batches (one for each color) with cold water and Soak®, or other products made especially for washing wool fabrics, and use a Shout® Color Catcher® dye-catching sheet to absorb any excess color that may leach into the wash water. Wash the natural skeins separately in the same way (without the sheet) to allow the yarn to bloom.*

Yarn Weight   Fingering, Superfine (CYCA 1)

Needles   Size 3 (U.S.)/3.25 mm 16-in. and 24-in. circular; 2 size 2 (U.S.)/3.00 mm DPNs, or size needed to obtain gauge

Stitch markers

Large-eye blunt needle

Notions   6 (6, 7) ½-in. yellow buttons

Matching sewing thread and needle

2 yd. ½-in.-wide orange twill tape

Pattern Sizes   Small (Toddler 2–4), Medium (Child 6–8), Large (Child 10)

Measurements   Skirt Width at Hem: 14 in. (16 in., 18 in.); Chest at Bodice: 24 in. (28 in., 32 in.); Length from Hem to Armhole: 14 in. (16 in., 18 in.); Armhole Length: 6½ in. (7 in., 7½ in.); Dress Length: 20½ in. (23 in., 25½ in.)

Pattern Difficulty   Advanced (uses steeks)

Fair Isle Gauge   8 sts = 1 in., 8 rnds = 1 in. on size 3 needles

Note   *For more about stranding, steeking, and cutting, see Techniques, page 22.*

Knitting Instructions

With Light Green and 24-in. size 3 circular needle, CO 224 (256, 288) sts. Without twisting the sts, join. Beginning of rnd is the center back of the dress.

Hem Facing

Work Rnds 1–5 of **In the Flower Garden Children's Dress Chart**.

FOLD RND

With Light Green, P.

NEXT RND

K.

Dress Skirt

Work Rnds 1–61 of **In the Flower Garden Children's Dress Chart**, then rep Rnds 30–61 as needed until skirt measures 12 in. (14 in., 16 in.).

BACK OPENING STEEK

Work sts in established patt to end of rnd, place marker, CO 10, alternating colors if it is a 2-color rnd. Beginning of rnd is now in the center of the back opening steek. (234, 266, 298 sts)

Work in established patt, working steek sts in alternating colors on 2-color rnds, following chart until skirt measures 13½ in. (15½ in., 17½ in.).

SKIRT DECREASE RND

With Natural, K5, move marker, *K5 (6, 7), K2tog*, rep around. (32 sts dec; 202, 234, 266 sts)

NEXT RND

K.

EYELET RND

K5, move marker, *K2, K2tog, YO*, rep around to marker, move marker, K 5.

NEXT RND

K, working each YO as a st.

ARMHOLE STEEK RND

K5, move marker, K47 (55, 63), place marker, K1, CO 8, K1, place marker, K94 (110, 126), place marker, K1, CO 8, K1, place marker, K46 (55, 63), move marker, K5. (218, 250, 282 sts)

NEXT RND

Work Rnd 1 of **In the Flower Garden Children's Dress Chart**.

Working steeks in alternating colors on 2-color rnds, work **In the Flower Garden Children's Dress Chart** Rnds 1–61, repeating Rnds 30–61 as needed, at the same time dec 1 st on either side of the armhole steeks only, every other rnd, 6 times. (24 sts dec; 194, 226, 258 sts)

Change to 16-in. circular needle if needed.

Work even in established patt until armhole reaches 6½ in. (7 in., 7½ in.).

Work 1 rnd in Natural.

BO all sts.

Steeks

Reinforce armhole and back opening steeks in your preferred method, according to the instructions in Techniques, page 26. Cut the steeks open. Fold the steeks in, and baste in place.

Shoulder Seams

Measure 3½ in. (3¾ in., 4 in.) from the folded armhole steek edge, along the upper edge, and mark. Sew the shoulder seams.

Back Neck Shaping

Measure down 1 in. from the upper edge in the center back on either side of the steek opening. Fold the upper edge down and in and pin in place, angling the fold up to the shoulder seam. Baste in place.

Front Neck Shaping

Measure down 2¼ in. from the center front upper edge and mark. Measure and mark an angled line from the center mark up to the shoulder seam. Sew a line of contrasting basting sts along this line. Sew a line of steek reinforcement sts ¾ in. up from the basted line, and cut the excess fabric away. Fold the neckline in and down along the basted line, and baste in place. Remove the basting.

In the Flower Garden Children's Dress Chart

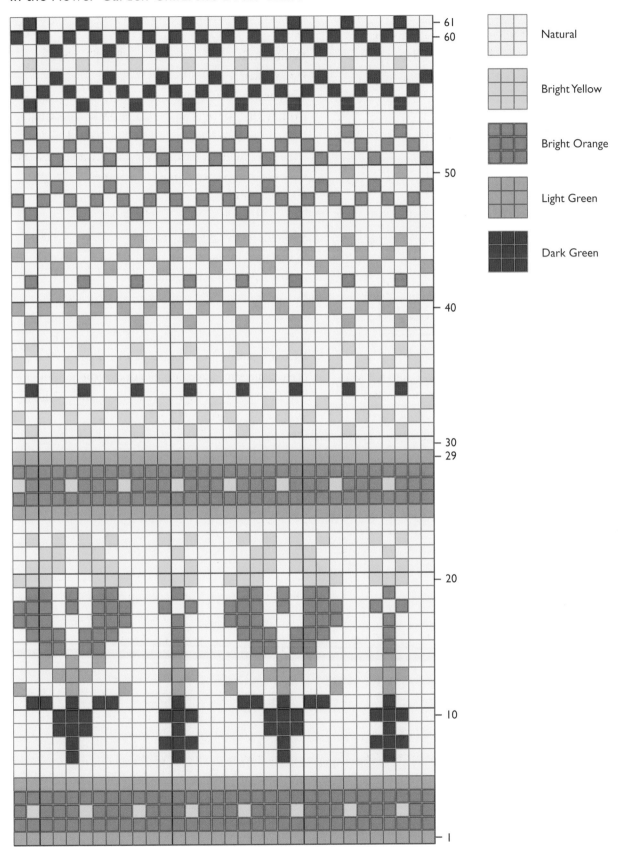

Natural

Bright Yellow

Bright Orange

Light Green

Dark Green

Armhole Edging (Applied I-Cord)

With Bright Orange and size 3 DPNs, CO 3.
Work from wrong side of lower armhole edge.

APPLIED I-CORD EDGING RND 1

Slide sts to right of needle, bring yarn around from behind the sts, K2, Sl 1 as if to knit, pick up and K 1 st from the folded armhole edge, PSSO.

Rep Rnd 1 around armhole opening, picking up each st in succession around the armhole opening, along the folded steek edge.

LAST RND

Slide the sts to the right, bring the yarn around from behind. Sl 1 as if to knit, K2tog, PSSO. Cut yarn, leaving an 8-in. tail. Pull the tail through the remaining loop and tighten.

Sew the ends of the Applied I-Cord Edging together. Weave the ends in. Rep with other armhole opening.

Neckline, Back Opening, and Buttonholes

Working from the wrong side, beginning at the top right back opening, and with Bright Orange, work an Applied I-Cord edging around neckline along the fold line, as for Armhole opening, until you get to the upper left neckline corner.

TOP BUTTONHOLE

Without cutting or tying the yarn off, slide the sts to the right, bring the yarn around from behind, and K across. Rep 6 more times, skip 2 sts along the folded back opening steek edge, and then work the Applied I-Cord Edging Row 1 as for the Armhole openings. Rep 9 times.

REMAINING BUTTONHOLES

Continue the buttonhole process of 7 rows of plain I-cord, skip 2 sts along the folded back opening steek edge, then work Applied I-Cord Edging for 10 sts, until 6 (6, 7) buttonholes have been worked. Work Applied I-Cord Edging to the bottom of the back opening. Finish and tie off as for the Armhole Edging.

Finishing

Weave all loose ends in on the inside of the dress. Sew the hem up and in along the purl fold line. Wash and block dress to proper measurements, and allow dress to dry. With matching sewing thread, sew the buttons in place along the back opening. Beginning at the back opening, using a large-eye needle, thread the twill tape through the eyelet openings, around to the back opening. Tie tape in a bow, and trim ends to desired length.

Tam

You should have enough yarn left from the *In the Flower Garden Children's Dress* to knit this adorable matching tam. (Pictured on page 8 knit in Decadent Fibers' hand-dyed, superwash sock yarn.)

Yarn Superfine Weight Yarn (CYCA 1), approx. 100 yd. each of Natural, Bright Orange, Bright Yellow, Light Green, Dark Green

Note *Hand-dyed yarns can sometimes bleed in the wash. Before knitting with them, wash hand-dyed yarns in separate batches (one for each color) with cold water and Soak, or other products made especially for washing wool fabrics, and use a Shout Color Catcher dye-catching sheet to absorb any excess color that may leach into the wash water. Wash the natural skeins separately in the same way (without the sheet) to allow the yarn to bloom.*

Yarn Weight Fingering, Superfine (CYCA 1)

Needles Size 2 (U.S.)/3.0 mm 16-in. circular; size 3 (U.S.)/3.25 mm 16-in. circular and DPNs, or size needed to obtain gauge

Stitch markers

Large-eye blunt needle

Dessert plate or saucer for blocking

Pattern Sizes Small (Toddler 2–4), Large (Child 6–10)

Measurements 8 in. (9¼ in.) across the top of the hat, lying flat and blocked

Note *Tam can be blocked either larger or smaller than listed above, depending on the plate used for blocking.*

Pattern Difficulty Beginner

Fair Isle Gauge 8 sts = 1 in., 8 rnds = 1 in. on size 3 needles

Note *For more about stranding, see Techniques page 22.*

Knitting Instructions

Note Small size will have 4 flower reps on the top of the tam, Large will have 5 flower reps.

With Light Green and 16-in. size 2 circular needle, CO 116 (140) sts. Without twisting the sts, join.

Ribbing

Work K2, P2 ribbing, 3 rnds each, in this order: Light Green, Dark Green, Bright Orange, Bright Yellow, Natural.

NEXT RND

Change to 16-in. size 3 circular needle. K with Natural, inc 12 (20) sts evenly spaced in rnd. (128, 160 sts)

Work **In the Flower Garden Tam Chart 1**.

Work **In the Flower Garden Tam Chart 2**, working the decs where shown on the chart. Work K2tog decs on the left side of the chart, and K2tog TBL on the right side of the chart.

Change to DPNs as needed.

RND 29

Sl 1, K2tog, PSSO, rep around. (8, 10 sts)

RND 30

K2tog, rep around. (4, 5 sts)

RND 31, LARGE SIZE ONLY

K2tog, K around.

Place all sts on one DPN.

I-CORD TOP ROW 1

Slide sts to the right side of the needle, bring the yarn around behind the work, and K across.

Rep I-Cord Top Row 1 four times.

LAST ROW

K2tog twice.

Cut yarn, leaving a 6-in. tail. Pull tail through remaining loops, tighten, and tie off on the inside of the tam. Weave all ends in on the inside of the tam.

Blocking

Soak tam and then squeeze or spin the excess moisture from the tam. Place the tam over a saucer (dessert plate), and pull so that the motifs are centered and even. Note that the tam can be blocked to either a larger or smaller size than listed in the pattern, depending on the plate used for blocking. Allow tam to dry, and then remove the plate.

In the Flower Garden Tam Chart 1

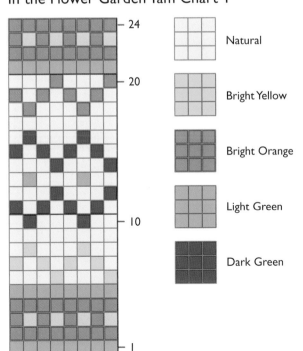

Natural

Bright Yellow

Bright Orange

Light Green

Dark Green

In the Flower Garden Tam Chart 2

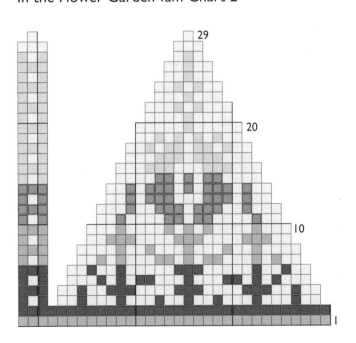

Children's Cardigan

Stroll through the flower garden with this lovely children's cardigan, worked in soft, hand-dyed blues and purples. (Pictured at right in Decadent Fibers' hand-dyed, superwash sock yarn.)

Yarn Superfine Weight Yarn (CYCA 1), approx. 800 yd. Natural and 400 yd. each of Dark Green, Light Green, Blue, Purple

Note *Hand-dyed yarns can sometimes bleed in the wash. Before knitting with them, wash hand-dyed yarns in separate batches (one for each color) with cold water and Soak, or other products made especially for washing wool fabrics, and use a Shout Color Catcher dye-catching sheet to absorb any excess color that may leach into the wash water. Wash the natural skeins separately in the same way (without the sheet) to allow the yarn to bloom.*

Note *There will be enough Light Green, Dark Green, Blue, and Purple left to complete the* **In the Flower Garden Children's Pants***.*

Yarn Weight Fingering, Superfine (CYCA 1)

Needles Size 2 (U.S.)/3 mm 16-in. circular needle, size 3 (U.S.)/3.25 mm DPNs and circulars in desired lengths, or size needed to obtain gauge

Stitch markers

Large-eye blunt needle

Notions Nine ½-in. buttons

Pattern Sizes Small (Toddler 2–4), Medium (Child 6–8), Large (Child 10)

Measurements Chest: 24 in. (28 in., 32 in.); Length to Sleeve: 8 in. (9 in., 10 in.); Cardigan Length: 14½ in. (16 in., 18 in.); Sleeve Length: 11 in. (12 in., 13 in.)

Pattern Difficulty Advanced (uses steeks)

Fair Isle Gauge 8 sts = 1 in., 9 rnds = 1 in. on size 3 needles

Note *For more about stranding, steeking, and cutting, see Techniques, page 22.*

Knitting Instructions

With size 3 circular needle and Light Green, CO 192 (224, 256) sts. Do not join. Turn.

HEM FACING RND 1 (RS)
K with Light Green, turn.

HEM FACING RND 2 (WS)
P with Purple, turn.

HEM FACING RND 3
K, turn.

HEM FACING RND 4
P, turn.

HEM FACING RND 5
K with Light Green, turn.
Fold Rnd 6 (WS)
K, turn.

SWEATER BODY RND 1
With Light Green, CO 5 sts, place marker, work Rnd 1 of **In the Flower Garden Children's Cardigan Chart**, place marker, CO 5, join. New rnd begins in center of center front steek. (202, 224, 256 sts)
Work steek sts in alternating colors on 2-color rnds. Work Rows 2–61 of **In the Flower Garden Children's Cardigan Chart**, and then repeat Rows 30–59 as needed, until sweater body measures 8 in. (9 in., 10 in.).

ARMHOLE STEEK RND
K 5 steek sts, alternating colors if a 2-color rnd, move marker, work 47 (55, 63) sts according to chart, place marker, K1, CO 8, alternating colors if a 2-color rnd, K1, place marker, work 94 (110,126) sts according to chart, place marker, K1, CO 8, alternating colors if a 2-color rnd, K1, place marker, work 47 (55, 63) sts, move marker, K5. (218, 250, 282 sts)
The sts between the new markers are the armhole steeks.
Continue working according to chart, working the steek sts in alternating colors on 2-color rnds, until armhole measures 6½ in. (7 in., 8 in.).
Work 1 rnd in Natural. BO all sts.

Sleeves (make 2)

With size 3 DPNs and Light Green, CO 66 sts for all sizes. Divide as desired, and without twisting sts, join.

HEM FACING
Work Rnds 1–5 of **In the Flower Garden Children's Cardigan Chart**.

FOLD RND
With Light Green, P.

SLEEVE
Work Rnds 1–5 of **In the Flower Garden Children's Cardigan Chart**.

NEXT RND
Inc 10 sts evenly spaced in Row 6 of **In the Flower Garden Children's Cardigan Chart**. (76 sts, all sizes)

NEXT RND
Begin Rnd 7, starting first patt rep at line indicated on chart for all sizes, work full reps after that, ending with a partial rep.

EVERY OTHER RND THEREAFTER
Inc 1 st at beg and end of rnd, until there are 108 (112, 128) sts while working chart, and then rep Rows 30–61 as needed. Change to circular needle as needed.
Work even, following chart, until sleeve measures 11 in. (12 in., 13 in.).

NEXT RND
K with Natural.
BO all sts.

Steeks

Prepare sleeve and center front opening steeks as described in Techniques, page 26. Cut the steeks open.

Shoulder Seams

Measure in 4½ in. (5¼ in., 5¾ in.) from cut sleeve steek edge and sew shoulder seams.

Back Neck Shaping

Measure and mark the center back neck opening. Fold the back neck edge in and down ¾ in. for all sizes, for

Continued on page 14

In the Flower Garden Children's Cardigan Chart

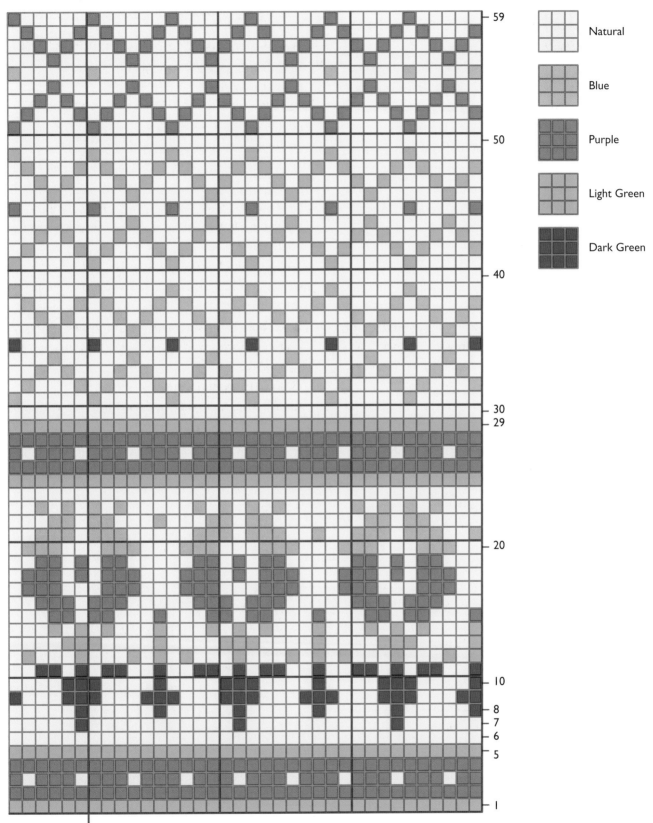

59
50
40
30
29
20
10
8
7
6
5
1

Natural

Blue

Purple

Light Green

Dark Green

All Sizes Sleeve: On Rnd 8 begin 1st repeat here, work full repeats thereafter, ending with a partial repeat

back neck facing. Gradually ease curve of facing up to shoulder seam. Tack in place.

Front Neckline Shaping (all sizes)

Measure 2 in. down from the upper edge, at the center fronts, and mark. Measure and mark a gradual matching curve from the center front up to each shoulder seam. With contrasting waste yarn, sew a line of basting sts along this curve. Measure 1 in. above the basting line, and mark. Reinforce along this line, as desired, for a neckline steek. Cut along front neckline steek reinforcement stitching. Fold neckline steek down and in along basting. Tack in place.

Left Front Band

Fold steek in. Beginning at top right side of right cardigan front at basting line, with size 2 circular needle and Light Green, pick up and K 104 (118, 136) sts evenly spaced to fold line. Turn.

ROW 1 (WS)

Work K2, P2 ribbing. Turn.

ROW 2 (RS)

Work K2, P2 ribbing. Turn.

ROWS 3–6

Change to Purple. Work K2, P2 ribbing. Turn.

ROWS 7–8

Change to Light Green. Work K2, P2 ribbing. Turn. BO in patt.

Right Front Band (Buttonhole Band)

Fold steek in. Beginning at bottom right front opening fold line, RS, with Light Green and size 2 circular needle, pick up and K sts as for Left Front Band. Work Rows 1–4 as for Left Front Band.

BUTTONHOLE ROW

Working as for Left Front Band, work 3 (6, 7) sts in established ribbing patt, *work 2 sts tog, YO, work 10 (11, 12) sts in the established ribbing patt*, rep, end with: work 2 sts tog, YO, work 3 (6, 7) sts in established ribbing patt.

NEXT ROW

Work as for Left Front Band, working each YO as a st. Finish as for Left Front Band.

Neckband

With size 2 circular needle and Light Green, pick up and K 100 (118, 134) sts along neckline folded edges, removing basting yarn as you pick up sts just below that line on the fronts. Turn.

Work and finish as for Left Front Band.

Fold all steeks in, and sew in place. Sew sleeves in place. Fold hem facings up and in and sew in place. Sew buttons in place. Weave all ends in on the inside of the sweater. Wash and block sweater.

Children's Pants

Knit these matching pull-on pants for younger children. (Pictured on page 11 knit in Decadent Fibers' hand-dyed, superwash sock yarn.)

Yarn Superfine Weight Yarn (CYCA 1), approx. 400 yd. each of Natural, Dark Green, Light Green, Blue, Purple

Note *Hand-dyed yarns can sometimes bleed in the wash. Before knitting with them, wash hand-dyed yarns in separate batches (one for each color) with cold water and Soak, or other products made especially for washing wool fabrics, and use a Shout Color Catcher dye-catching sheet to absorb any excess color that may leach into the wash water. Wash the natural skeins separately in the same way (without the sheet) to allow the yarn to bloom.*

Note *There should be enough of the Light Green, Dark Green, Blue, and Purple left from the* **In the Flower Garden Children's Cardigan** *yarn requirements to complete the pants. You will need a whole skein of Natural to complete the pants.*

Yarn Weight Fingering, Superfine (CYCA 1)

Needles Size 3 (U.S.)/3.25 mm 16-in. circular needle and DPNs, or size needed to obtain gauge

Stitch markers

Large-eye blunt needle

Notions ¾ yd. ½-in.-wide elastic

Pattern Sizes Toddler's 2 (4)

Measurements Waist: 24 in.; Leg Length to Crotch: 10 in. (12 in.); Length from Crotch to Waist: 8½ in. (9½ in.); Pants Length from Waist to Leg Hem: 18½ in. (21½ in.)

Pattern Difficulty Advanced (uses steeks)

Fair Isle Gauge 8 sts = 1 in., 9 rnds = 1 in. on size 3 needles

Note *For more on stranding, steeking, and cutting, see Techniques, page 22.*

Knitting Instructions (make 2)

Note Size 2 and 4 are knit with the same number of sts; the size difference is in the leg and waist length.

With size 3 DPNs and Light Green, CO 64 sts. Making sure the sts aren't twisted, join.

LEG CASING RNDS 1-5

K with Light Green.

LEG FOLD RND 6

P.

NEXT RND

K.

Leg

Work Rnds 1–5 of the **In the Flower Garden Children's Cardigan Chart.**

RND 6 OF CHART

Inc 8 sts evenly in rnd. (72 sts)

RNDS 7-29 OF CHART

Work according to chart.

LEG INCREASE RND 1

Continuing with chart, inc 1 st at the beg and end of the rnd. (2 sts inc)

LEG INCREASE RND 2

Follow chart.

Rep Leg Increase Rnds 1–2 until there are 96 sts. Change to circular needles as needed.

Work even, following chart, repeating Rows 30–61 as needed, until leg measures 10 in. (12 in.) from the Leg Fold Rnd.

Steek

Work to end of rnd in the established patt, following chart, place marker, CO 10 sts, alternating colors if it is a 2-color rnd.

New rnd begins in center of the newly cast-on steek sts. Work the 10 steek sts in alternating colors on 2-color rnds. Steek will be the center front and center back pants seams.

Work even in established patt, following chart, until the piece measures 8½ in. (9½ in.) from the beginning of the steek.

Waist Casing

FOLD RND

With Natural, P.

WAIST CASING

K. Work 1 in. even with Natural.

BO all sts. Weave all loose ends in on the wrong side of the fabric.

Pants Assembly

Prepare steeks as described in Techniques, page 26. Cut the steeks open.

Fold the steeks in and baste in place. Sew the pants sections together along the center front and back steeks.

Leg Finishing

Fold the leg casings up and in along the P fold line, and sew in place.

Waistline Finishing

Fold the waist casing in and down along the P fold line and sew in place, leaving a 1-in. opening. Thread elastic through the casing, tightening as desired. Cut and sew the elastic together. Sew the 1-in. opening closed. Wash and block pants.

Children's Cardigan

The Geometric Dazzle motif is so versatile that it works in subdued as well as bright colors. Knit this zipper-front children's cardigan in worsted weight, with superwash yarns for ease in laundering. (Pictured on page 20 knit in Knit Picks Swish™ Worsted.)

Yarn Medium Weight Yarn (CYCA 4), approx 220 yd. each of Dark Green, Pink, Brown, White; 110 (110, 220) yd. Tan; 110 yd. Light Green

Yarn Weight Worsted, Medium (CYCA 4)

Needles Size 7 (U.S.)/4.5 mm 16-in. circular, size 8 (U.S.)/5 mm DPNs, 16-in. and 24-in. circulars, or size needed to obtain gauge

Large-eye blunt needle

2 large stitch markers

4 small stitch markers

Notions 12-in. (14-in., 16-in.) black separating zipper

Sewing thread and needle

Gauge 5.5 sts = 1 in., 6 rows = 1 in. on size 8 needles

Sizes Child Size 2 (4, 6)

Blocked Measurements Chest: 24½ in. (26½ in., 28½ in.); Back Length: 14½ in. (16 in., 17½ in.); Sleeve Length: 10 in. (11 in., 12 in.)

Pattern Difficulty Advanced (uses steeks)

Notes *For more about steek preparation, cutting, and general information, see Techniques, page 22.*

The beginning of the round is in the middle of the center front steek. Tie on new colors at the beginning of the round.

If you are using superwash yarn it will not felt, so the cut edges on the steeks will look a little more ragged than in projects worked with yarns that felt when washed.

Knitting Instructions

Sweater Ribbing

With a 24-in. size 8 circular needle and Pink, CO 134 (146, 158) sts. Being careful not to twist the sts, join.

RND 1

Tie on Brown. Work the first 5 sts alternating Pink and Brown, place large marker. Following the **Ribbing Chart**, work K2, P2 corrugated ribbing, working the K sts in Pink and the P sts in Brown. Work to within 5 sts of the end of the rnd, place large marker, and work the rem 5 sts alternating Pink and Brown. The 10 sts between the markers will be the center front steek. Work 6 rnds of ribbing as per the **Ribbing Chart**, working all of the Pink sts in K, and the Brown and Tan sts in P.

Sweater Body

Beginning where indicated on the **Geometric Dazzle Children's Cardigan Chart**, work the sweater body as shown until it measures 8 in. (9 in., 10 in.).

NEXT RND (ARMHOLE STEEK)

K5, move marker, K28 (31, 34), place small marker, CO 10 sts (alternating colors if it is a 2-color rnd), place small marker, K68 (74, 80), place small marker, CO 10 sts (alternating colors if it is a 2-color rnd), place small marker, K28 (31, 34), move marker, K5. The 10 sts between each new set of markers will be the armhole steeks. (154, 166, 178 sts)

Work even for 4 in. (5 in., 6 in.).

Neckline

RND 1

Work to within 12 (14, 15) sts of the last center steek marker, BO those 12 (14, 15) sts, remove marker, BO rem 5 sts of the rnd.

RND 2

BO the first 5 sts, remove marker, BO the next 12 (14, 15) sts, work to the end of the sts, replace marker, CO 5 sts for the steek, alternating colors if it is a 2-color rnd.

RND 3

Tie on new colors if indicated by the chart border you're working on. CO 5 sts, alternating colors if it is a 2-color rnd, replace marker, work around. (130, 138, 148 sts) Work even until armhole steek measures 6½ in. (7 in., 7½ in.) and sweater body measures 14½ in. (16 in., 17½ in.).

Bind off all sts.

Finish the armhole steeks as desired, and cut them open. Finish the center front steek as desired, and cut it open. Fold the cut steeks in and pin or tack in place if necessary.

Fold the small neckline steek in. Using a yarn color from the last knitted border, sew the sweater back and front together at the shoulders, from the armhole steek to the shoulder neckline edge (as indicated by the folded neckline steek).

Sleeves (make 2)

With Brown and a 16-in. size 8 circular needle, and beginning at the lower armhole edge, pick up and K 70 (76, 82) sts evenly spaced around the armhole. Place marker at beginning of rnd.

RND 1

K with Brown.

Begin knitting charted patterns where you left off from the Sweater Body. You may mix and match the border patterns if you like. Do not worry if the pattern reps don't match up at the beginning and end of the rnd.

SLEEVE DECREASE RND 1

K2tog, K, working in established chart motif to within last 2 sts, K2tog.

SLEEVE DECREASE RND 2

K, working in established chart motif.

Rep these 2 rnds until there are 30 (32, 32) sts left. Change to DPNs as necessary. Work even in established chart motif until sleeve measures 8 in. (9 in., 10 in.). Work ribbing as for Sweater Body for 2 in. BO sts loosely in patt. Weave all loose ends in on the inside of the sleeve. Whipstitch the armhole steeks in place on the inside of the sweater.

Continued on page 21

Geometric Dazzle Children's Cardigan Chart

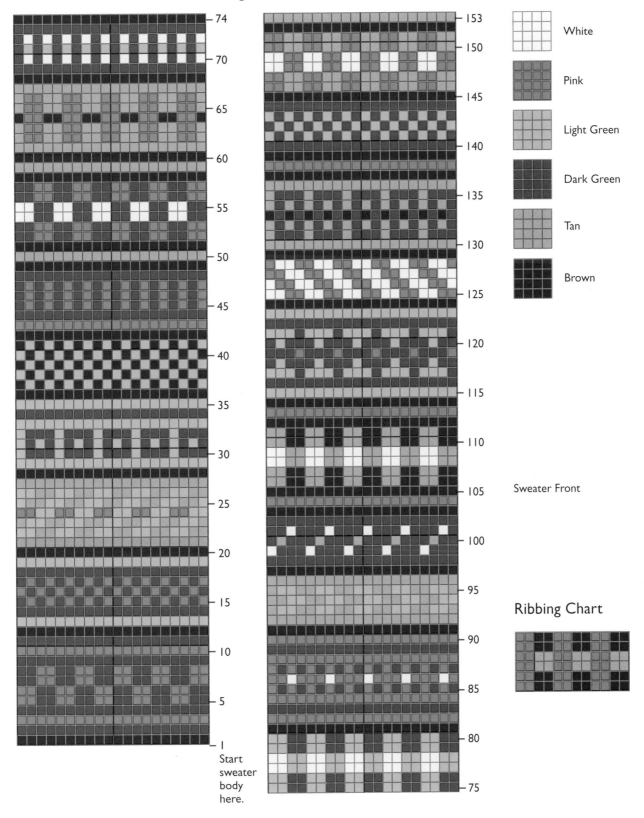

Sweater Front

Start sweater body here.

White
Pink
Light Green
Dark Green
Tan
Brown

Ribbing Chart

Front Band

With a 16-in. size 8 circular needle and Pink, pick up and K 74 (78, 86) sts evenly spaced along the right side of one front edge.

BAND ROW 1 (WS)

Work as for Sweater Ribbing, P the Pink sts, K the Brown sts. Turn.

BAND ROW 2

(RS) Work as for Sweater Ribbing, K the Pink sts, P the Brown sts. Turn.

BAND ROWS 3–4

Rep Band Rows 1–2 with Tan and Pink.

BO in ribbing with Pink.

Rep with other front band.

Whipstitch the center front steeks in place on the inside of the sweater. Weave in all loose ends.

Neckband

With a 16-in. size 7 circular needle and Pink, pick up and K 90 (94, 98) sts evenly spaced around the neckline, including the front bands.

Work ribbing as for Front Bands. BO in ribbing with Pink.

Whipstitch the front neckline steeks in place on the inside of the sweater. Weave in all loose ends.

Wash and block the sweater to the listed measurements.

Zipper

Pin the zipper in place along the center front openings. Hand- or machine-stitch the zipper in place.

Techniques

Let's start with knitting increases and decreases, which is something that tends to bedevil beginners. The experienced among you may have your own approach, so do what you know to work best.

Increases

I like to increase stitches by picking up and knitting the side loop from the stitch in the row directly below the row I am working on. This increase does not leave a hole in my knitting. There are other types of increases. Use the one that you prefer, but be consistent. Use the same increase throughout.

Left-Slanting Decreases

Unless otherwise noted, any decrease indicated on the right side of a chart will be a left-slanting decrease. In other words, it's a decrease where the combined stitches lean toward the left.

The slip, slip, knit (SSK), in which you slip the first stitch as if to knit, slip the second stitch as if to knit, then slide the left-hand needle into the front part of both stitches and knit them together, makes a nice left-slanting decrease.

You may use an SSK for any left-slanting decrease in this book. However, I prefer to knit two together through the back loop (K2tog TBL), which produces the same effect with less effort. Simply slip your right needle into the back side of the two stitches, and knit them together. Whether you use an SSK or a K2tog TBL, be consistent. Use the same left-slanting decrease throughout any given project.

Right-Slanting Decreases

Unless otherwise noted, any decrease indicated on the left side of a chart will be a right-slanting decrease. In other words, it's a decrease where the combined stitches lean toward the right. Work all right-slanting decreases by knitting two stitches together in the usual way (K2tog).

Changing Yarn Colors the Fearless Way

There are many "official" ways to change yarn colors at the beginning of a round, which is where you switch colors on most Fair Isle projects. The fearless way is just to cut the former color, leaving at least a 3-in. tail. Then tie the new color to the old color with a plain old square knot, leaving at least a 3-in. tail on the new yarn color, and continue knitting.

That square knot will loosen a bit as your knitting progresses, and sometimes the first and last stitches of those rounds will look a little loose as well. Don't worry about them.

After you finish your project, when it comes time to weave your loose ends in (the ends that aren't trimmed off when the steek is cut open, that is), use a needle to further loosen and untie the knot, pull on the ends a bit to tighten the adjacent stitches, and retie the square knot firmly. Then weave the ends in along the wrong side of the knitted row for an inch or so, and trim the excess tail.

I have never had a knot tied in this manner come undone in wearing or washing. The small knots don't show from the front of the fabric, nor do they make lumps on the wrong side (in socks, for instance).

An added bonus is that tightening the yarn ends often makes that "jog" that happens at the beginning of color-change rounds disappear entirely.

Speaking of that Jog

There are ways to eliminate the jogs that occur at the beginning of a round of striped or Fair Isle knitting. I don't worry about them—I consider them the nature of the beast.

Joining Same-Color Yarns the Fearless Way

If you need to join more yarn to a same-color round (for example, if you're working on a project with large areas of single color) you can tie the yarn ends together, as listed above.

But even more fearlessly, if you are using a yarn that can be felted (wool or wool blends that are not superwash), you can *spit-join* your yarn ends together.

I know this sounds a bit ooky, but it works: Put the end of the old yarn and the end of the new yarn in your mouth (just go with me here), and roll them around for a moment or two. Get them good and wet. Take the yarns out of your mouth, overlap the ends a couple of inches lengthwise, and squeeze them together to form a single strand. Place the strand with the wet portion on one palm. Place the other palm on top and rub your hands together vigorously until the yarn strands felt together (you can feel when that happens).

Then just knit. The join will hold. I promise. In addition, felting reduces the bulk of that short area of double stranding. It won't show from the front (or back) of your work. And once the yarn dries, you'll never be able to find the join again.

If you're really squeamish, you can wet the yarn ends with tap water, but that means getting up and going to the sink. It's easier to do it the totally fearless way.

Yarn Dominance and Ball Placement

It is important in Fair Isle knitting to pick up your strands in the same order throughout your project. I place my main or background color (MC) on the right arm of my chair or beside me, and the contrast color (CC) on the floor or in my lap in front of me, and keep that placement throughout. I am a "thrower." I have learned that some "pickers" prefer to place the CC on the arm of their chair, and the MC in front. Do whatever works for you, but be consistent. Don't change the placement of the balls in the middle of the project.

There are some Fair Isle knitters who twist the yarns around each other on every stitch. I don't recommend that—it not only takes time and uses up a lot more yarn, but the resulting fabric is stiff.

Do not twist the strands around each other unless you are knitting more than five to seven stitches of the same color in a row on the chart, depending on the yarn weight. You can go up to seven stitches with fingering weight yarn without twisting the strands. If you do have to twist the yarns in the middle of long stretches of the same color, untwist them on the next stitch, so that the original ball placement/strand orientation returns. Your finished piece will have uniform stitching and color "dominance" if you maintain the same strand order throughout.

Knitting from a Chart

Each square on a Fair Isle chart represents one stitch. The color of the square represents the color yarn you are supposed to use for that stitch.

Each pattern will specify where to begin on the chart. Some projects begin at the top row, right-hand square of the chart. Others begin at the bottom row, right-hand square of the chart.

Some sizes of some patterns will indicate a different place to begin your first pattern repeat. Individual instructions will specify where to begin working those charts.

One row of squares on the chart equals one repeat of the motif. Each time you finish a repeat of your pattern round, go back to the first stitch and start over for the next pattern repeat on your round.

I find it extremely helpful to place markers between each repeat. That way, if I make a mistake, I only have to go back to the beginning of the repeat to find the error.

Each row of squares on the chart represents one round of knitting. When you finish one complete round of repeats, begin the next round on the far right square in the row up (or down, depending on where you started working) from the one you just completed.

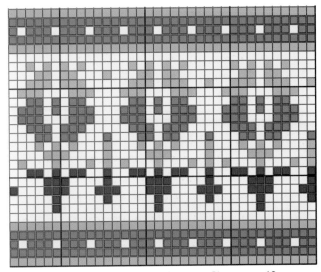

In the Flower Garden Children's Cardigan Chart, page 13

I don't just find it helpful to mark which round I am knitting on a chart, I find it absolutely essential to do so. There is no chart so simple that I cannot lose my place in it, thereby causing angst and anguish, wasted work, and many bad words. I eliminate that possibility by using a metal sheet and strip magnets to highlight the chart row I am working on, with the magnetic strip placed just above my current row. If you don't have a metal sheet and strip magnets, you may use sticky notes in the same way. You can also photocopy the chart and use a highlighter to draw through each completed row.

Charted Decreases

Some project charts have decreases built right into them (the In the Flower Garden Tam Chart shown below, for example). Those charts look something like a pyramid, with the numbers of squares (and stitches) in a repeat gradually diminishing. The charts will have clearly visible jogs on decrease rounds. Each decrease is represented by a clearly delineated jog in the chart. When you come to a jog, you simply decrease one stitch (with either a K2tog TBL or a K2tog, depending on the side of the chart where the decrease falls), using the yarn color shown in the square.

Each decrease reduces the number of stitches in the repeat (and therefore in the entire project).

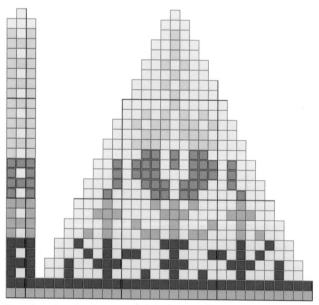

The decreases are built right into the In the Flower Garden Tam Chart.

Changing to Double-Pointed Needles

Unless you are using the Magic Loop method, or are knitting with two long circular needles, as you work on any pattern with decreases, you will have to switch from longer circular needles to shorter ones, and from circular needles to double-pointed needles (DPNs). Or, conversely, if you are working from the cuff up, on sleeves, for example, you'll start with DPNs and then switch to circulars as the stitch count increases. Use whatever circular length feels comfortable to you (changing them as necessary), and switch over to DPNs as needed.

If at all possible, place an entire pattern repeat (or multiple repeats) on separate DPNs. Be aware that your tension and gauge may change a bit in the switch to DPNs. If you find yourself knitting tighter on DPNs, move up a needle size.

Holding the Yarn Strands for the Floats

There are many ways to hold the yarn strands in Fair Isle knitting. The one that is correct is the one that works best for you. I hold both strands of yarn in my right hand. Other knitters hold one strand in their left hand and one in their right. However you hold your yarn, arrange the yarn balls as instructed earlier.

For beginners, I recommend holding only the strand that you are knitting with. When you finish the stitches for that color, drop that strand and pick up the other and knit those stitches without twisting the yarns around each other. After you feel comfortable switching colors, try holding both of the strands in one hand, or one strand in each hand. Experiment until you find the method that feels the most comfortable to you.

Float Tension

It takes practice to achieve even float tension when Fair Isle knitting. As mentioned above, I find it easiest for beginners to hold only the strand they're actually knitting with, then drop that strand and pick up the next color (as indicated on the chart), and loosely pull it up to the needle and continue knitting.

Even the best Fair Isle knitters get some puckering—don't worry if you see some in your work. As long as your knitting will stretch (test the elasticity occasionally), you should be able to block the puckers out. As you knit and get used to the process, you will find that your float tension relaxes on its own.

Twisting the Yarn Strands in the Float

Unless you are knitting a stretch of more than five to seven stitches of the same color in a motif, it is not necessary to twist the yarn strands around each other as you knit. If you do knit more than five to seven stitches in the same color on a row, at about the middle of that section of stitches, twist the "live" yarn around the "other" strand once and knit a stitch. Then untwist the yarn and continue on. This method produces a nicely elastic fabric, with a good drape.

It is common for a hint of the twisted stitch to show from the front of the fabric. If the chart has large areas of single-color stretches that extend over several rows of squares, stagger your twisted stitches so that they're not directly above or below each other to lessen their visibility on the right side of the work.

Weaving In the Ends

If your project involves steeking, many of your yarn ends will be cut away and discarded when the steek is cut open. (Yay!)

But for sleeves knit one at a time, and for pullover sweaters and vests, as well as hats, mittens, and socks—that is, for any tube that is not cut open—every color change involves yarn ends that will have to be woven in. It's boring, but it has to be done.

After retying the knots, thread one yarn end in a large-eye blunt needle (choose a needle that is only as big as it needs to be to fit the yarn through the eye). Working horizontally along a nearby row of stitches, on the wrong side of the fabric, weave the yarn end over and under several of the purl bumps (or over and under adjacent floats). Do this for about an inch. Trim the yarn end.

Repeat until you are finished with all of the yarn ends, or until you run screaming into the night, whichever happens first.

Weaving in ends

Wet Blocking

Wet blocking allows your yarns to bloom, stretch, and even out for a beautiful finished project. There are many products specifically produced for blocking and washing hand knits, but I use dish soap.

To wet-block small items, run a sink full of hot water. Add a small amount of dish soap and stir it around until the water is mildly sudsy. Submerge your item in the hot, soapy water, and allow it to soak for at least a half hour. Do not agitate the item, unless you want it to felt. Drain the water, and rinse in clear water no cooler than the soaking water. Gently squeeze the excess moisture from the item (rolled up in a towel), or put it in the spin cycle of your washing machine (do not agitate). After the excess moisture has been removed, smooth your item out. You may be able to just smooth it to the proper dimensions given in the pattern. Smooth the fabric, tug at any puckers, pull edges and sides even. Be sure to check the front, back, top, and bottom of the item, and smooth and tug as needed.

When it meets your approval, simply lay it flat somewhere and allow it to air-dry (I usually leave everything, from socks to sweaters, on top of my dryer overnight).

If the item will not smooth or unpucker properly, you may stretch the fabric, and then use nonrusting pins. When I pin-block an item, I usually just pin it to my living-room rug (as long as I know that the yarn that will not bleed or run). You may want to invest in a blocking board.

Be careful when pinning your item—any portions pulled out of shape will remain that way after the pins are removed. Allow the item to dry and remove the pins.

To wet-block large items, repeat the above steps, soaking the item in the washing machine or a large bucket or basin, or even in the bathtub. Be very careful not to let the washer go into agitation.

It is possible to add about 10 percent to the height and width of a knitted item by careful blocking, so if your piece is too small, you can widen and lengthen it at this stage.

Blocking only lasts as long as the item remains dry. You will have to reblock your item every time it is washed or gets wet in any way.

Laundering

Even if your item has been knit with superwash wool that is absolutely machine washable and dryable, you'll want to launder it exactly as for the blocking process. Machine washing superwash Fair Isle items leaves them shapeless and lumpy.

Steeks

For knitting purposes, a steek is a built-in seam allowance, which allows knitters to make Fair Isle projects entirely in the round, without having to work back and forth or purl stranded designs. The steek is cut open after the knitting is finished and additional shaping is done (such as curved necklines) or pieces (like sleeves) are added.

The biggest fear a knitter has, when cutting that first steek, is that the fabric will unravel. I won't pretend that can't happen, but as long as you use the right kind of yarn (with some grab) and don't play tug-of-war with your freshly cut knitting, those steek stitches won't go anywhere you don't want them to go.

Yes, it's scary the first time you take scissors to your knitting. I will admit to drinking a glass of wine before I cut my first steek. These days, I don't even think about it (outside of measuring many times before cutting). The ease of working a sweater tube in the round far outweighs any fear of cutting into the knitting, which is a fabric, just like any other.

Steek Construction

Some knitters like to use an uneven number of stitches in their steeks, and then cut down the middle of the center stitch when they open the steek. I prefer to use an even number of stitches and cut between the center two stitches.

Center-front steeks, for cardigans, are built into the original number of cast-on stitches (the first and last five stitches of the round composing the steek). Regardless of any stitch patterning on the body of the sweater, including textured stitches, ribbing, or cables, the steek stitches are always plain knit stitches.

Armhole and V-neck steeks are added to the construction at the right spot in the knitting by casting on a set number of stitches. Those stitches then become the steek, and they are worked the same way a center-front steek is worked.

In all cases, work your steek stitches in alternate colors on two-color rounds, except for the center two stitches, which are worked in the same color to make them easier to identify when it comes time to reinforce the steeks for cutting.

Steek Reinforcement

CROCHETED STEEKS The advantage of a crocheted steek is that you don't need any complicated machinery to do the work for you. You can crochet a steek on the bus or while standing in line at the post office. The disadvantage of a crocheted steek is that the crocheted edge adds bulk to the steek.

To make a crocheted steek, find and mark the center row of stitches along the length of your steek (easy to discover if you have worked those center stitches in the same color, as recommended above). Using a contrasting fine yarn (smaller than the yarn used to knit the project) and a properly sized crochet hook, begin at the top, working a single crochet through the center of the middle stitch. Then work a single crochet from the center stitch, and one through the stitch directly beside it on the steek row. Continue making single crochets down the entire steek side. Cut and tie off the yarn, and repeat on the other side.

Uncut crocheted steek reinforcement

Uncut hand-sewn steek reinforcement

Machine-sewn steek

HAND-SEWN STEEKS You can reinforce a steek by working hand-sewn cross stitches with fine yarn or thread, catching each loop on either side of the center row of steek stitches, as with the crocheted method.

MACHINE-SEWN STEEKS (MY PREFERRED METHOD) While I have used both the crocheted and hand-sewn steeking methods, when I reinforce a steek (either before or after cutting—more about that later), I use a sewing machine.

Find and mark the center row of the steek stitches, as described earlier. Adjust your sewing machine to the widest zigzag stitch possible and an average stitch length, loosen the pressure on your presser foot, and carefully zigzag-stitch along the center of the steek on both sides. Be careful not to stretch the fabric as you sew.

Steek Cutting

Eeek!

Okay, now that you have that out of your system, calm down and get ready to cut.

If the area being cut is one that is not easily delineated by the steek itself (such as front neckline shaping), measure again. This cannot be emphasized strongly enough: *Be absolutely certain that you are cutting in the right place.*

Then take your scissors and slowly, carefully snip open the steek between your reinforcements (whatever style you use). Trim any excess yarn ends from the edge.

See, it wasn't that hard!

Your newly cut steek should not unravel, especially if you have zigzagged the edges with your sewing machine, but just for safety's sake, don't pull on the steek anyway.

Cut the stitches between the reinforcement of this crocheted steek.

Cutting a hand-sewn steek

If you like, you can zigzag (or hand-stitch) over the new raw edge, but it's not absolutely necessary. You can now fold your steek in, baste it in place (if called for in your pattern), and continue on.

Fearless Steeks

You might want to cut a few steeks in the ways outlined above before trying this, but here is what I do: I just cut the steek open, without reinforcing it in advance.

Yep, you read that right. I just take my scissors and cut the steek open, and then I use my sewing machine to zigzag-stitch along the newly cut edges.

I have never had a steek unravel. Nope, not even once.

However, I will add this caution, which you should take very seriously: *Do not try this method with slippery yarns (cotton, silk, or most man-made fibers).* You can only "cut first, reinforce later" on projects knitted with yarn that adheres well (wool or wool blends).

Also, don't wait around after cutting an unreinforced steek open. Take it directly to the sewing machine (or hand-sew) the raw edges.

If the Unthinkable Happens

It is not likely, but if your cut steek does unravel, don't panic. Stop, take a deep breath, and examine the ravel. Determine where it starts and where it ends.

With a needle and thread (not yarn), anchor as many of the loose loops as you can by hand. Then use your sewing machine to zigzag the area and reinforce the weak spot. If necessary, use leftover project yarns to duplicate-stitch over the raveled area and any weak spots on the right side of the fabric.

Sleeves, the Sort-of-Fearless Way

Traditionally, sleeves are knit into the armhole opening on Fair Isle sweaters by picking up stitches at the opening and working your way down the sleeve, ending with cuff ribbing.

It's a good method, and one that can be adapted to almost any of the sweater patterns in this book, but that's not the method I generally use because flipping the entire sweater over after every round as I knit is a pain. The sweater is heavy (and hot), the weight slows the rest of the knitting down, and manhandling the entire sweater while knitting both sleeves exponentially increases the chance that the fabric will get dirty, stained, or snagged.

I much prefer to knit the sleeves separately, then sew them in place. The time I lose in sewing those two seams is more than made up for in the convenience of not constantly flipping the whole sweater around as I knit the sleeves.

The cut edge of a hand-sewn steek

The cut edge of a crocheted steek, right side

The cut edge of a crocheted steek, wrong side

Tandem Sleeves, the Totally Fearless Way

So you hate knitting two sleeves, you say? What a pain it is to cast on (or pick up) stitches and knit the same thing twice!

I agree. That's why I don't knit sleeves consecutively. I knit them together.

That's right, I knit both sleeves at the same time, and not with the Magic Loop sock method (knitting each tube separately, on the same set of needles).

For tandem sleeves, I knit each cuff separately, then I place them on a single circular needle, casting on 10 stitches between the sleeves as steeks, with markers on either side of both of the new steeks (that's 20 new stitches for the steeks). Then I join them, and, from that point, I work the sleeves in the round, increasing before the markers as though I was working each sleeve separately.

When I finish the sleeves and bind off the large tube (which will likely have more stitches than there were in the body of the sweater), I just cut them apart through the center of the steeks (it's difficult to machine-reinforce the steek before cutting tandem sleeves apart), zigzag along the cut edges, fold the steek edges in, and sew the long sleeve seam.

Picking up stitches for the shaped neckline along the basted line

Granted, you will have to sew that seam, which you would not have to do if you knitted each sleeve separately as a tube. On the other hand, if you knitted the sleeves separately, you'd have to weave about a bazillion ends in. With tandem sleeves, the yarn ends are cut away when the sleeves are cut apart!

The patterns in this book are written for more traditional sleeve construction, but you may adapt most of the sleeve instructions to this method.

After working tandem sleeves in the round, cut apart the steek.

Picking Up Stitches

Many Fair Isle patterns have front and neck bands that are picked up and knit along folded steek edges. When you pick up a stitch, insert the left needle through both loops of the base stitch, and knit those loops with the right needle. The new stitch goes on the right needle, and is now live.

Pick up and knit the number of stitches instructed in each pattern.

Picking Up Stitches the Fearless Way

Except in a very few cases (buttonhole bands, for example, or bands that have Fair Isle patterning, or need multiples of four stitches for ribbing), it really doesn't matter if you pick up the exact number of stitches listed in the pattern for neck bands, armhole openings, or front bands. A few more or less won't make a difference.

While you can pick up one stitch for each horizontal stitch or vertical row in a piece of knitting, you can often get by with fewer stitches. A rule of thumb if you're not counting the picked-up stitches, is to pick up four stitches for each five rows of vertical knitting. Along horizontal stretches, four stitches for each five stitches works as well. It's a matter of guessing and judging when you pick up stitches along a curved neckline.

Do keep track of how many stitches you pick up on armholes and front bands, so that you pick up the same number on the other opening.

Shaping Necklines

For the most part, the necklines (front and back) of the projects in this book are shaped after the piece has been knit and is off the needles.

Back necklines are shaped by folding the upper edge between the shoulder seams in and down to form a facing.

Round front necklines are shaped by marking the line where stitches will be picked up, then excess fabric is cut away above that line, and the cut edge is reinforced (or that line is reinforced before cutting). The front neckline is then folded in and down.

Neckband stitches are picked up along the basted line (see photo on page 29).

Contrasting thread is used for basting stitches along the neckline.

Machine-sewn neckline that has been cut for shaping

Stitches transferred to circular needle

V-neck shaping can be done by decreasing stitches at the center front, with a new cast-on steek in between the decreases. The steek is cut open and folded in, and the neckband stitches are picked up in the same manner as a round neck band, except that decreases are performed on either side of the V point so the band will lie flat.

Fearless V-neck Shaping

If you've read this far, you probably knew this was coming: You can put in a V-neck after the body tube is knit, just by cutting down the center front of the sweater or vest to the proper depth. You will have to take extra care to reinforce the row of stitches directly below the cut so they don't unravel, but that isn't difficult.

Then just fold your V-neck in at the angle that pleases you best, trim the excess, zigzag along the cut edge, and proceed as for a V-neck that was shaped by steeking and decreases.

Fearless Shaping in General

In fact, you can do all of your shaping after the sweater or vest body tube is knit. Decide where your sleeves should be (location, depth, and so on), shape the front neckline (round or V-neck), make the shoulders more narrow—almost any shaping (except making the piece bigger) can be decided on and performed after the body is knit.

Bear in mind that you will still need to fold under about a half inch of knitted fabric for armholes, front bands, and neckline shaping, so you may need to adjust your sleeve length or front band width to compensate for that loss.

Fearless Fixing

Okay, so you're done with your project, and you spot an error in your Fair Isle patterning.

The first thing you have to decide is whether it's worth addressing—I mean, if you finished the entire sweater and didn't notice until now, then it's not a terrible mistake, right? You may just want to ignore it and resist the urge to point it out to passersby, who will also not notice the mistake if they're not guided directly to it.

But if you can't live with it, and it's too late to rip the knitting out, there are a couple of things you can do to fix small patterning errors.

DUPLICATE STITCH Use the proper yarn color and a large-eye needle and duplicate-stitch over the mistake(s).

PERMANENT MARKERS Yeah, you read that correctly. If the error has been worked with a light yarn, you may just be able to color it with the proper darker shade of permanent marker. I don't recommend doing this for large areas, but trust me, no one will ever know if you fix a stitch here and there this way.

So there you have it.

You now know everything you need to knit Fair Isle, fearlessly and happily. What are you waiting for? Get those needles out and get busy!

Look for these other THREADS Selects booklets at www.taunton.com and wherever crafts are sold.

Baby Beanies
Debby Ware

EAN: 9781621137634
8 ½ x 10 ⅞, 32 pages
Product# 078001
$9.95 U.S., $11.95 Can.

Fair Isle Flower Garden
Kathleen Taylor

EAN: 9781621137702
8 ½ x 10 ⅞, 32 pages
Product# 078008
$9.95 U.S., $11.95 Can.

Fair Isle Hats, Scarves, Mittens & Gloves
Kathleen Taylor

EAN: 9781621137719
8 ½ x 10 ⅞, 32 pages
Product# 078009
$9.95 U.S., $11.95 Can.

Lace Socks
Kathleen Taylor

EAN: 9781621137894
8 ½ x 10 ⅞, 32 pages
Product# 078012
$9.95 U.S., $11.95 Can.

Colorwork Socks
Kathleen Taylor

EAN: 9781621137740
8 ½ x 10 ⅞, 32 pages
Product# 078011
$9.95 U.S., $11.95 Can.

DIY Bride Cakes & Sweets
Khris Cochran

EAN: 9781621137665
8 ½ x 10 ⅞, 32 pages
Product# 078004
$9.95 U.S., $11.95 Can.

DIY Bride Beautiful Bouquets
Khris Cochran

EAN: 9781621137672
8 ½ x 10 ⅞, 32 pages
Product# 078005
$9.95 U.S., $11.95 Can.

Bead Necklaces
Susan Beal

EAN: 9781621137641
8 ½ x 10 ⅞, 32 pages
Product# 078002
$9.95 U.S., $11.95 Can.

Drop Earrings
Susan Beal

EAN: 9781621137658
8 ½ x 10 ⅞, 32 pages
Product# 078003
$9.95 U.S., $11.95 Can.

Crochet Prayer Shawls
Janet Severi Bristow & Victoria A. Cole-Galo

EAN: 9781621137689
8 ½ x 10 ⅞, 32 pages
Product# 078006
$9.95 U.S., $11.95 Can.

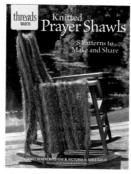

Knitted Prayer Shawls
Janet Severi Bristow & Victoria A. Cole-Galo

EAN: 9781621137696
8 ½ x 10 ⅞, 32 pages
Product# 078007
$9.95 U.S., $11.95 Can.

Shawlettes
Jean Moss

EAN: 9781621137726
8 ½ x 10 ⅞, 32 pages
Product# 078010
$9.95 U.S., $11.95 Can.